ARIADNE'S
THREAD

To Felicity

ARIADNE'S THREAD

Polish Women Poets

Translated and Introduced
by

Susan Bassnett
and
Piotr Kuhiwczak

FOREST BOOKS/UNESCO
LONDON ☆ 1988 ☆ BOSTON

UNESCO Collection of Representative Works
European Series

This book has been accepted in the translations
collection of the United Nations Educational Scientific
and Cultural Organisation (UNESCO)

Published by Forest Books
20 Forest View, Chingford, London E4 7AY, U.K.
PO Box 438, Wayland, M.A. 01788, U.S.A.

First published 1988

Jacket Design © Jolanta Marcolla
English Translations & Introduction © UNESCO
Photographs © Danuta B. Lomaczewska
Original work © Authors' Agency, Warsaw

Cover design & setting by Ann Evans

Typeset in Great Britain by Cover to Cover, Cambridge
Printed in Great Britain by A. Wheaton & Co Ltd, Exeter

British Library Cataloguing in Publication Data
Ariadne's thread: Polish women poets.
1. Poetry in Polish. Women writers, 1919–
Anthologies
I. Bassnett, Susan.   II. Kuhiwczak,
Piotr
891.8'17'0809287

ISBN 0–948259–45–0

Library of Congress Catalog Card Number
88–080462

Contents

Kazimiera Illakowiczówna

Maria Pawlikowska-Jasnorzewska

Anna Świrszczyńska

Anna Kamieńska

Wislawa Szymborska

Urszula Kozioł

Acknowledgements

Apart from volumes of poetry by individual poets, the following anthologies have been used by the authors:

Kolumbowie i współcześni. Edited by A. Lam
Warsaw 1972.

Ze struny na strunę. Edited by A. Lam
Krakow 1980.

Poeta pamięta. Edited by A. Barańczak
London 1984.

The following poems have appeared in *Writing Women* (Vol. V, No. 2, 1987)

'A Meat Recipe' by Urszula Kozioł
'Ariadne's Thread' by Maria Pawlikowska-Jasnorzewska

Introduction

There are some countries whose literatures enjoy world wide fame, whose writers are translated into a vast number of different languages and sometimes even appropriated into the literary canon of other cultures. And there are other countries whose literatures, however magnificent and varied, remain mysteriously unknown, whose writers remain strangely unfamiliar, no matter how great their reputation may be in their homeland. Czeslaw Milosz, one of the best known Polish writers of this century, uses the image of the white space on the map to describe the world's acquaintance with his native culture. The map of Europe, he argues, consists of the Great Cultural Powers, with everything else fading away into whiteness, with blurred edges. Poland, with its rich cultural history and complex, versatile language occupies a vaguely defined space somewhere to the East of the Germans and West of the Russians. At times of crisis, when the eyes of the world follow political changes rather than literary ones, attention may briefly shift onto the undefined areas of the map, but then it moves away again. The great wealth of Polish poetry remains unknown to millions of readers.

In deciding to assemble a collection of contemporary Polish poetry, we faced a double difficulty. On the one hand, the absence of a tradition of translation for Polish poetry into English meant that English language readers might be unfamiliar with even the best known Polish poets. On the other hand, the huge output of poetry meant that any process of selection was bound to be difficult. Moreover, the cultural gap between the English speaking world and Eastern Europe in terms of the reading of poetry is so huge that it makes one gasp. In the former, volumes of poetry appeal to a minority public and are sold and read in tiny numbers, whilst in the latter new editions of poems are printed and sell out in tens of thousands of copies. Poetry in Poland has an immediacy and a dynamic that is unthinkable in the English speaking world, where it tends to have restricted appeal.

As we began our work, reading through the output of a large number of twentieth century Polish poets, we began to find ourselves attracted more and more to writing by women. Perhaps, since one one of us is a woman and a poet herself, this was almost inevitable, but increasingly we came to believe that a collection of contemporary Polish women's poetry would provide English language readers with an opportunity to experience for themselves the best of Polish writing today. Of course, there are plenty of excellent Polish male poets, several of whom are well-known outside Poland (Zbigniew Herbert or Tadeusz Rozewicz, for instance) but the women seemed to us to have an energy and an immediacy that captured and held our imagination as readers.

It is significant that Poland is often referred to as female in English. 'She' has suffered invasions, occupation, destruction and rebirth and, unlike some nations which English resolutely describes in the masculine, femininity and Poland have been equated. This figurative language conceals the patronising attitude so often adopted towards Poland and not only in this century either. Poor Poland, the victim, the tender defenceless female with her great, flat plains laid open beneath the jackboots of invading armies, is an image that can be summoned up at the convenience of those powers who at other times chose to forget that Poland exists at all. And yet, as always happens when a nation or a culture or a language is marginalized, from that position of marginalization outside the power arena, comes intense exuberance and experimentation in art. No revolutionary artistic movement, no new dynamic in creative expression, ever came from the established culture, but always from the outer limits. So it has been with Polish writing: ignored by the great powers of Europe, Poland has produced a long line of brilliant, exciting and different writers, and the sufferings that the Polish people have undergone have fuelled the creative imagination of writers.

Within Poland, the power of the Church has been strongly felt, sometimes as a repressive influence, at other times as a liberating one. As with so many Latin American writers, of whom Cesar Vallejo and Pablo Neruda are good examples, the language of religion combines with political awareness to create a whole new style, a poetry that is both very clear and at the same time densely coded. The Transubstantiation which lies at the hear of Catholic dogma, offers us a chance to believe that something which is bread and wine on the Communion altar is not really itself but is actually something other, the sacrificial body and blood of Christ. This metaphor has provided generations of poets with an alternative mode of thinking: the poet may talk about one thing,

about one concrete object, and the reader may then transub-
stantiate the poem into something else. What is said is
meant, but there is hidden meaning too. It is no accident
that surrealism has flourished in Polish literary history, and
many writers use surrealistic techniques to express feelings
that are very definitely rooted in the real world.

If Polish history and culture has been marginalized by the
rest of the world, then Polish women are doubly marginal-
ized. The rebirth of feminism in the Sixties and the advent
of feminist criticism has shown all too clearly that women
writers have failed to gain the status accorded to their
female counterparts. Countless women poets have vanished
altogether, and countless others have been marked as lower
in talent or output. Socialist countries have been
endeavouring to redress that balance, but without much
thought and subtlety. Thus old habits die hard and
patriarchy as an ideology is a powerful force on both sides of
the East–West divide. However, we have been struck by the
extraordinary energy of so many women writing in Eastern
Europe generally – the poets of Poland, Rumania and the
Soviet Union, the novelists and short story writers of the
GDR for example, and the growing numbers of women
working in the alternative theatre in Poland, Czechoslo-
vakia and Hungary, all of which points to the emergence of
a female creativity that transcends patriarchal structures
and expectations of the official scene.

As we looked at Polish women poets, we were struck by
the recurrence of themes and images that also recur in the
work of women writers in other cultures – by the blending
of public concerns with private pain, the return to classical
mythology, the emphasis on smallness rather than on vast-
ness. This collection, which consists of poems by eight
women (and might well have consisted of the work of
eighteen or more, had we the space and finance) aims at
providing a representative selection of twentieth century
Polish women's poetry. Many of the writers share the same
themes – a sense of bewilderment about the purpose of life,
determination to struggle against pain, the need to define
themselves as women, with women's voices in a male
world. So Halina Poswiatowska, in her poem 'Whenever I
really want to live I cry . . .', depicts life as a lover trying to
desert her. Anna Świrszczyńska uses the image of washing
as a sign of being alive and healthy. Maria Pawlikowska-
Jasnorzewska asks simply when did a mermaid ever need a
life belt? ('Security'). Like their male counterparts, Polish
women poets are deeply concerned with history, though

with the place of the individual in the vastness of history rather than with an abstraction. 'I am back to simple things', says Kazimiera Illakowiczowna ('The Return'), whilst Urszula Kozioł suggests that it is time to return to not-knowing ('Return to Not Knowing'), and Anna Kamienska says that we do not have any history, 'we only have moments of wasted life' ('History').

Waste is a powerful motif in many of the poems in this collection, waste through war (and images of war feature strongly, particularly in the work of Anna Świrszczyńska, Ewa Lipska and Wislawa Szymborska), waste through lack of love, waste through the oppressive passing of time. But through the pain and cynicism there are powerful notes of hope. 'I will be back', says Maria Pawlikowska-Jasnorzewska ('Ariadne's Thread'), holding onto Ariadne's ball of string as she crosses into exile before Hitler's invading forces, and although in fact she never was able to return, the assertion and hope in her poem challenge the forces of death. Anna Świrszczyńska celebrates her own ageing, proclaiming her independence and her grey hair as she runs past amused strangers on a beach ('Running on the Beach'). And Wislawa Szymborska can still praise dreams and see visions in clouds and announce that she prefers defeated nations to the defeating ones, even though she reminds us of the constant presence of death, torture and repression in the world today, as there has always been throughout time. The strength in the voices of these poets compel us to listen and take note of what they say.

A collection like this is necessarily the tip of an iceberg. Great acres of poems are still to be translated. The choice of poems, finally, was a personal one. We have translated those poems which we both related to and which we felt spoke to us. Other translators may well have chosen a completely different selection of writers and of poems, and there may be those who feel that we should have paid attention to canons of literary greatness, rather than reliance on personal taste. But we believe that the function of poetry is that of sharing experience; what we shared with the original writers, with the eight women included in this book, we hope to share with our English language readers. And maybe this process of sharing will make the white space of Poland a little more colourful and delineate more sharply the lines blurred by the bias of history.

Translators' Preface

The translation of the poems included in this anthology has taught both of us a great deal about the processes of transferring texts from one language into another. In the past we had both worked separately as translators, so the first task that we faced was to decide on a practical working method that would enable us to use our special skills. We each brought something to the translation process that the other did not possess: Piotr Kuhiwczak as a native Polish speaker was able to pinpoint nuances and patterns of foregrounding in the source poems that a non-native speaker might never have seen, whilst Susan Bassnett had been writing and publishing her own poetry for some years and therefore had a sense of what would and would not work in English as a poem.

We both shared a common concern with the status of translation, and had both contributed through teaching and writing to the developing discipline of Translation Studies. We both believe that translation is a serious art, involving detailed knowledge of the source and target cultures and we also believe that for too long translation has been looked down on by so-called 'original' writers and practised by people who have often not been sufficiently well-qualified to tackle the job in hand. Separately, neither of us would have dared to attempt the translations contained in this book, but working together we felt that we complemented one another and compensated for each other's inadequacies.

Our starting point was a principle of translation that involved not rigid ideas of 'faithfulness' to the originals but rather creative unfaithfulness. By this, we mean that although we attempted to convey the shape of each original poem along with its tone and mood, we agreed from the outset that certain qualities would inevitably be lost. The sound patterns of Polish are too far removed from those of English to be imitated or reproduced, so we agreed to dispense with rhyme or to try to hunt for words with similar consonant clusters. Nevertheless, we felt that the principles of syllabic structuring in Polish poetry could be reproduced in some approximately similar way in English, and we took care to establish syllabic patterns in the metre of the English versions. We also felt that repetition as a structural device was as essential to the translation as to the source text and wherever patterns of repetition occured, we endeavoured to create such patterns in our translation.

We worked as a team from the outset; Piotr would produce an initial close version, whilst Susan would produce an initial crude approximation of the tone and content of the Polish text using only her very rough acquaintance with the Polish language. Then we put both these versions together, and revised our separate readings. Time and again we found that Susan had discovered the fundamental structures and mood of the poem, even though there were gaps in her overall understanding, which raised questions in our minds as to where meaning in a poem can be said to lie. If a sense of the meaning of a poem is obtainable from an understanding of the poem's structure despite inadequate linguistic knowledge, this raises again some of the unresolved questions first posed by critics half a century ago.

The next stage of the translation process involved Susan's reworking of Piotr's revised literal version. Here also we found certain unexpected changes occuring. Piotr had taken pains to put this version into what he felt was good English, and at times he had altered word order, even altered the order of lines in the interest of what he felt was linguistic fluidity. In every case, Susan changed these lines and restored the original Polish order, in the interest of what she felt was the proper foregrounding of poetic devices. So whilst Piotr carefully transformed the language into familiar structures and patterns. Susan then carefully defamiliarized it. The conclusion that we came to through the lengthy process of translating the poems in this way, is that the particular qualities of language that made these poems work in Polish somehow struggled through into English, despite the huge differences in syntactical and semantic order between the two languages. In short, that their poeticity, if we can use such a term, crossed the boundary of language. If this is indeed the case, we see it as an immensely positive sign of great hope for the future; politicians may stockpile nuclear weapons, but the voice of the poet speaks out to us all.

Susan Bassnett is currently Senior Lecturer in charge of
Comparative Literature at the University of Warwick.
She has published several books, the most recent
being *Feminist Experiences (The Woman's Movement in
Four Cultures)* Allen and Unwin 1986; *Sylvia Plath*
Macmillan 1987; and *Elizabeth the First* Berg 1988, and
has worked as a journalist, actress, translator and
interpreter. She has been publishing poetry for many
years and runs the Writers' Workshop Programme at
Warwick.

Piotr Kuhiwczak divides his time between the
University of Warsaw and the University of Warwick.
He is a well-known translator and has written
extensively on Romanticism.

The Poems

Kazimiera Illakowiczowna
(1892–1983)

Kazimiera Illakowiczowna was born in Vilno (Lithuania). After her parents' death she moved to Vitebsk and Warsaw, then studied literature in Petersburg, Krakow and Oxford. When the Great War broke out, Illakowiczowna was in Russia, where she worked first as a nurse, then in one of Petersburg's publishing houses. She went back to Warsaw at the end of the war as a civil servant in the Ministry of Defence and Foreign Affairs. She published her first volume of poetry in 1912 in Krakow. Between 1926 and 1935 she was personal assistant to the Polish political leader, Marshal Pilsudski. At the outbreak of the Second World War she left Poland, and found asylum in Transylvania where she taught foreign languages and translated German and Hungarian literature into Polish. She came back to Poland in 1947 and settled in Poznan to work as a freelance writer. Illakowiczowna's output consists of more than ten volumes of poetry, literary essays and memoirs.

Major editions of Illakowiczowna's works:

Wybor wierszy (Selected poems), Warszawa 1956.
Wiersze zebrane (Collected poems), Warszawa 1971.

Kazimiera Iłłakowiczówna

Leaves are falling on us

Sometimes I have a dream:
I am buried in yellow leaves
beside the great porch of eternity.
Damp, slimy trees feed the soil,
I sense the winter's roots
sleeping below me.

Sometimes I have a dream:
we are buried in yellow leaves
— roots, sand, grass and me.
I will not let go, nor tear the shroud,
I will stay in the cathedral porch
like a stone on a river bed.

A sea of leaves above me,
then a shuttered church.
Sometimes a dream like this comes
on the eve of eternity.

Kazimiera Iłłakowiczówna

Illusions and reality

A heart promised to break.
It was not broken.
Life threatened to wither.
Nothing faded it.

So what has happened?
Is all this real?
Petrified in poetry
it stays alive.

Poetry

You cannot drink her, nor eat her.
No, I do not like poetry!
She has sharp thorns,
her sticky coating oozes,
she threatens with sediments.
You wait and wait, but she sheds nothing.

If only she desired to break through.
But all she does is deceive.
She is like useless glue.
Oh, let's try to forget her,
maybe she will dissolve . . .
No, I do not like poetry.

The return

I am back to simple things — to the dance of dust in air,
to a tiny sightless spider coloured like the wall,
to bitter, sobbing blinds that shiver in the cold,
to strange slits in the floorboards full of powder and
$$\text{puzzles.}$$

I am back from a hard, triumphant journey, from a
$$\text{crusade,}$$
to the secret mousehole hidden in a corner,
to the dreadful death of a woodchuck, to the hedgehog's
$$\text{fright,}$$
to escapes beyond belief of owls and bats.

Things are quieter now, easier, brighter, safer.
I am back like a weary dragon to the old, old tale.

Death
First version

Before there was no death,
then her shadow grew with mine,
later she was put in a corner
like a rolled papyrus . . .
Today she is close by and quick witted,
each of my days accounts for her,
she waits close by me and mine
like an uncut book.

There is no old age

There is no old age! Only fruit and a flower,
and new wheat, and a seed and everything starts afresh.
Because the same angel, either in frost or early spring
spreads his youthful wings, and grows and grows and
grows!

Maria Pawlikowska-Jasnorzewska
(1893–1945)

Maria Pawlikowska-Jasnorzewska was born in Krakow; her father was the well-known painter Wojciech Kossak, and she studied at the Academy of Fine Arts. Her first volume of poetry entitled *Niebieskie migdaly* (Blue Almonds, 1922) was not well received by leading critics who claimed that it was too 'feminine'. For some time she belonged to the 'Skamander' group of poets in Warsaw, one of the leading literary circles in inter-war Poland (1918–1939). When Hitler invaded Poland in 1939, Pawlikowska-Jasnorzewska managed to cross the Romanian border, joining the Polish forces in France and later in Britain. After the war she settled in Manchester where she died in 1945. Pawlikowska-Jasnorzewska published more than ten volumes of poetry in Poland and Britain but some of her poetry and plays still remain unpublished.

Major editions of Pawlikowska-Jasnorzewska's works:

Poezje (Poems), Warszawa 1976.
Wiersze wybrane (Selected poems), Warszawa 1985.

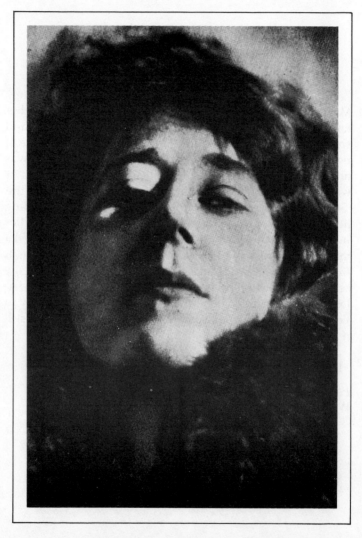

Maria Pawlikowska-Jasnorzewska

Old age

The hazel grove has put on purple satin,
a lime tree wears a gown of silky green.
But I shall not change again,
no-one will look at me.

There are strange men
who make bundles of nettles and weeds
but where are the ones
who would kiss an old woman's hair?

I am alone.
Grandmother, they call me —
I feel like a dark spot
on the bright-hued rug of the world.

Grandma

In fifty years' time she'll sit down by the piano
(she'll be seventy four by then),
a grandma, wearing jumpers,
who lived through a long, very boring war.
A grandma who saw trams in the streets,
saw a plane take its first steps in the sky,
heard people speak on the telephone
without seeing each other.
A grandma recalling old legends,
who remembers Pilsudski and Foche,
who loved jazz bands
who collected letters from postmen,
and who wasted her young life, never owning
a biophone, helicycle, astrodact, or pediter.
Watching a faded film, nostalgia makes her smile
and she plays an old-fashioned foxtrot.

Security

Are you worried about me? Why?
Yes, life is stormy and infinitely evil,
but when did a mermaid ever need
a life belt?

Maria Pawlikowska-Jasnorzewska

Letters

Into the fire with my love letters!
Into the fire, quickly with my papers!
Since flames inspired you
flames shall be your shroud!

Ariadne's thread

Down in Zaleszczyki along Rybacka Street
is the Ariadne hotel. The nearby hills were spread
against the sky in a tapestry blush
of honest, autumn colours.
Shallow and sleepy, the Dniester crept along
and cut off Polish tragedy from Romanian silence.
Up in the cloudy sky a monastery reared like a clump of
                    bluebells.

At dawn you couldn't see the sun in the abyss,
but by nine o'clock it cleared the hurdles proudly
like a golden horse in slow, gleaming leaps.
The lazy waters brightened unexpectedly
and slowed down further. Shimmering leaves
brought by the wind fell into the border waters
and the neighbouring land. Roses shed petals
across gardens. Poland was withering.

The Ariadne hotel was the last place I stayed
in the Country. After that I entered
the Labyrinth. But may the name of Ariadne
be a good omen for me. I am holding the ball —
the string is fixed to the threshold. I will be back.

Anna Świrszczyńska
(1909–1984)

Anna Świrszczyńska was born in Warsaw. She studied medieval and baroque literature at university. Her first poems were published in literary magazines in the early 1930s, but her first volume of prose poems appeared in 1936. During the Second World War Świrszczyńska took an active part in the Warsaw Uprising (1944), and it was her war experience which had the greatest impact on her second volume of poetry *Budowalam barykadę* (Building the Barricade, 1972). Her last volume of poetry entitled *Cierpienie i radość* (Suffering and Joy) was published in 1984. Świrszczyńska died in the same year. Selections of her poetry have been recently published in Britain and America.

Major editions of Świrszczyńska's works:

Wybor wierszy (Selected Poems), Warszawa 1980.
Building the Barricade, Krakow 1979. A bilingual edition.
Happy As a Dog's Tail, Harcourt Brace Jovanovich, San Diego, 1985.
Fat Like the Sun, Women's Press, London 1986.

Anna Świrszczyńska

A woman writer
doing her washing

Enough typing for today.
Right now, washing
in the old style.
Wash, wash, rinse, wring,
like my grand and great grandmothers.
Relax.

Washing is healthy and useful
as a laundered shirt. Writing
is suspicious.
Like three question marks
typed on paper.

He did not jump down
from the third floor

The Second World War.
Warsaw.
Last night they dropped bombs
on Theatre Square.

My father's workshop
is in Theatre Square.
All his paintings, work
of forty years.

This morning he went
to Theatre Square.
He realized.

His workshop had
no roof
no walls
no floor.

My father did not jump down
from the third floor.
My father just began all over again.

I do not accept

I do not accept
my fingernails
that grandfather once grew,
nor my head occupied
for the last two thousand years
by Caesar's bloody corpse.

The dead
are straddled on my mountainous back.
The carrion, body and soul
of barbarous ages
rots in me.
Cruel corpses of past times
want me to be
as cruel as they were.

But I shall not repeat
their deathly words.
I must give birth to myself
anew. I must give birth
myself to my new age.

Poetry reading

I lie down, curled up
like a dog
chilled to the bone.

Who can tell me
why I was born,
why the horror called life
goes on.

Suddenly the phone. I am
off to do the reading.

I arrive.
A hundred people, two hundred eyes.
Watching. Waiting.
I know what for.

I am to tell them
why they were born,
why the horror called life
goes on and on.

Running on the beach

I am running on the beach.
People are puzzled.
— Grey hair but running.

I am running on the beach
with an insolent expression.
People are laughing.
— Grey hair but insolent.
I feel accepted.

When I dig potatoes

I am digging potatoes for dinner.
An ant has climbed up
my bare leg.
— Ant, what do you think
of eternity?

The ant's head is superhuman,
like chemical reactions
in the sun.
The ant can teach me
all about the eternal questions.

Digging potatoes
is good for the mind.

Two hundred and eighty degrees below zero

When I am alone
there is more room inside me.
I sit down comfortably
inside me, with my legs crossed,
and settle down to thinking
about this and that.

When I am alone
every religion's paradise
blooms in me.
Splendours and wings float
upwards.

When I am alone
the frost of outer space
pierces through my skin.
Two hundred and eighty degrees
below zero.

Anna Kamieńska
(1920–1986)

Anna Kamieńska was born in Krasnystaw (Eastern Poland). First she trained as a teacher, and in the 1940s she attended literature seminars at the underground Warsaw University. After the Second World War, Kamieńska read classics at the Catholic University in Lublin and then in Łodz. In the late 1940s and through the 1950s she worked as a literary editor on several periodicals. She started her literary career with a volume *Wychowanie* (Education) published in 1949. For twenty-five years she worked as a freelance writer and translator. She translated from Latin, French, Bulgarian, Russian and Serbo-Croatian. Her original output consists of more than fifteen volumes of poetry, three novels, some collections of literary essays and many poems and stories for children. Her works have been published in France, Czechoslovakia, Bulgaria, Israel, the Soviet Union and Germany.

Major editions of Kamieńska's works:

Poezje wybrane (Selected poems), Warszawa 1971.
Wiersze (Poems), Warszawa 1982.

Anna Kamieńska

Heaven

I used to believe that justice would be done.
So I did not cry when my hair was pulled,
I suffered silently the unjust slap in the face,
slander both visible and invisible,
lost belongings, my burned doll,
the war which came instead of youth,
the handbag stolen from me,
my bicycle confiscated forever,
the old people's home, full of strangers,
the causeless quarrel, that thief called death,
loneliness I did not deserve,
a catalogue of injustice in which I was lost.
And I wait and wait
for my vast tears to be wiped away
by the all-embracing Father, nothingness.

Little Dorrit

Little Dorrit waited for me under the Christmas tree,
smelling of new print.
She slept with me in my bed
sharing my dreams
snuggling under my pillow.
Then she was lost in wartime,
with no glory, like my other things.
But her spirit, the Nike of Childhood
soared in her frock
out over smoke and flames.
Long ribbons in her bonnet,
tiny feet in buttoned boots
swooped overhead,
'Wait!' I shouted,
but she flew off and vanished
into Dickensian mists
into the maw of the fireplace
beneath a blanket of snow.

History

We do not have any history
we only have moments
of wasted life.
We only have forty eight hours
of false justice.
This is not history, nor her bells,
these running sands, subdued voices,
our funerals in whispering leaves,
a hug over the coffin and eyes, eyes . . .
Time, rolling over us,
does not have the brow of history,
just the shrewd, sharp muzzle of a fox.

Cosmic wrappings

Swaddled in spaceship cabins
they appear on television screens
like grandparents long since dead
called back from the underworld.
In that restricted space
the way hands move amazes;
if, in the shining universe of time
we saw the hand of Leonardo
suspended with a brush
or the fingers of Giordano Bruno
protruding from the stake,
none of that would surprise us.
The announcer would say clearly:
Now here you can see
the hand of Leonardo
being raised
to paint the Last Supper.
And now, a glimpse of
Giordano Bruno's fingers
as he burns to death in Rome.
Thank you for your attention.
We shall be back with you after the break.

The key

A small boy wears a key
round his neck on a string.
A symbol of homelessness.
He carries his empty home,
where he can return any time
but he will not go back because
empty houses do not make homes.
Don't lose it, said his mother, leaving.
Dinner is in the oven.
One day he will lose the key,
he will wander as if in a dream,
he will pluck at his chest.
It was there, on thick string.
A small boy with a key.
I meet him on my way
and cannot help him at all.
I lost all my keys too.

Loving my enemies

At last I have some real enemies
and I should start by loving them;
we have even signed a secret pact of difference.
Possibly you might mistake us
for two sides of the same coin,
or two ends of the stick.
Our coats hang in the cloakroom side by side,
we speak the same words
though our languages are quite dissimilar,
conjunctions divide us and do not join.

It is prudent even to love bad weather,
since, after all, it is weather of some sort.
I hunt for a point on the map of being
where two human lights at least can find some
                                        rest.

Caught in two feeble beams
they yield to love with slowness.

Lord, you know how hard it is,
and that finally judgement will be passed.
Justice shrinks before the fact
that people are afraid of one another.
If they were magnificent wild beasts
it might be worthwhile dying in their argument's claws
              but
              enemies must be loved to the bitter end
              of our mortal truth.

Given away

I have given away everything,
all the favourite things
of everyone dear to me,
even the stone
from the Aegean Sea.
I never regretted
those broken plates
nor my roses and trees.

Now, sitting here, I wonder
whether Someone Great thinks
I still have a lot
to give away.

Wislawa Szymborska
(born 1923)

Wislawa Szymborska was born in Kórnik (Western Poland). In 1931 she moved with her parents to Krakow, and in 1945 went to the Jagiellonian University to study literature and sociology. Her first volume of poetry *Dlatego zyjemy* (That's What We live For) was published in 1952. In 1953 she became the poetry editor of the Krakow weekly *Zycie Literackie* (Literary Life), where she published some of her poems and numerous book reviews. She lives and works in Krakow. Szymborska is probably the best known Polish woman writer in the English-speaking world.

Major editions of Szymborska's works:

Wiersze wybrane (Selected poems), Warszawa 1964.
Peezje wybrane (Poems), Warszawa 1967.
Poezje (Poems), Warszawa 1970.
Ludzie na moscie (People on the Bridge), Warszawa 1986.
Sounds, Feelings, Thoughts: Seventy Poems by Wislawa Szymborksa, Princeton University Press, 1981.

Wislawa Szymborska

Options

I prefer cinema.
I prefer cats.
I prefer oaks beside the Warta.
I prefer Dickens to Dostoyevski.
I prefer myself loving people
to myself loving mankind.
I prefer to have needle and thread close by.
I prefer greeness.
I prefer not to state
that reason is responsible for things.
I prefer exceptions.
I prefer to leave early.
I prefer to chat with doctors about trivia.
I prefer old faded illustrations.
I prefer to be ridiculous writing poems
than to be ridiculous and not write.
I prefer loving anniversaries
which are celebrated every day.
I prefer moralists
who promise me nothing.
I prefer clever kindness to the naive variety.
I prefer this earth without uniforms.
I prefer defeated nations to defeating ones.
I prefer to have reservations.
I prefer the hell of chaos to the hell of order.
I prefer Grimm's tales to newspaper headlines.
I prefer leaves without flowers to flowers without leaves.
I prefer dogs with untrimmed tails.
I prefer light eyes, since mine are dark.
I prefer drawers.
I prefer many things not mentioned here
to many others unmentioned.
I prefer zeroes randomly scattered
to zeroes lined up in rows
I prefer a time of flies to a time of stars.
I prefer to touch wood.
I prefer not to ask how much longer and when.
I prefer consideration of the option
that there are many ways of being.

Wislawa Szymborska

Tortures

Nothing has changed.
A body feels pain,
it must eat and sleep and breathe air,
it has thin skin with blood beneath,
it has a substantial number of nails and teeth,
its bones are fragile, its joints quite pliable.
All this is significant during torture.

Nothing has changed.
A body suffers as it did
before and after the founding of Rome,
in the twentieth century before and after Christ.
Tortures are all the same, only the world shrinks and
everything that happens is always somewhere else.

Nothing has changed.
Only there are more people,
new offences have been added to old ones,
real, presumed, temporary and nonexistent,
yet the scream a body responds with
has been, is and will be innocently
in the same old scale and key.

Nothing has changed.
Maybe manners, rituals, dances have,
but the movement of shielding the head is still the same.
A body writhes, twists, struggles,
collapses and buckles when knocked off its feat,
blackens, swells, spits and bleeds.

Nothing has changed.
Except the shape of frontiers,
the borders of forests, shores, deserts, icebergs.
Brooding in such landscapes,
the soul comes and goes, flickers near then far,
a stranger to itself, impalpable,
unsure perhaps of its existence,
while body just is, is and is
and does not know where to go.

To the Ark

Heavy rain has just begun to fall.
Come into the ark, where else can you go:
poems for one voice only,
private rejoicings,
talent not vital,
curiosity unnecessary,
a tiny range of grief and horror,
willingness to look in six different ways.

Rivers swell and their banks overflow.
To the ark: light and shade, half tones,
whims, trimmings, tit-bits,
foolish exceptions,
forgotten signs,
countless shades of grey,
a game for the game's sake,
a tear of laughter.

Water and mist, as far as sight can stretch.
To the ark: plans for a distant future,
joy over differences,
admiration for winners,
choice limited by more than two options,
old fashioned scruples,
time for thoughts,
and trust, that all this
may be useful again.

For our own sakes,
being children still
tales have happy endings.
Anything else would be out of key.
It will stop raining,

the waves will die down,
the clouds will open
to a radiant sky
and be ordinary above our heads:
sublime and trivial
looking like
happy islands,
lambs,
cauliflowers,
and babies' nappies
drying in the sun.

Children of this age

We are the children of this age,
this age is political.

All your, his, our
day and night-time affairs
are political affairs.

Whether you like it or not
your genes have a political future
the colour of your skin is political
your eyes have a political dimension.
Whatever you say has its echo
whatever you keep quiet about
is political regardless.

Apolitical poems are political too
the moon in the sky does not look like the moon.
To be or not to be, that is the question.
What question, tell me, my darling?
The political question.

You need not even be a human being
to acquire political importance.
It is enough just to be oil
fodder or recyclable material
or a conference table, the shape of which
can be on an agenda for months.
All this time people have been dying
animals have been starving
houses have been burning
fields have been turning fallow
just as in far off distant
less political ages.

In praise of dreams

In my dreams
I paint like Vermeer van Delft.

I speak fluent Greek
and not only with the living.

I drive a car
that does what I say.

I am talented,
I write epic poems.

I hear voices
no less often than saints do.

You would be amazed
at my skill in piano playing.

I fly properly
all by myself.

Sliding off the roof
I fall onto soft grass.

I do not find it hard
to breath under water.

I cannot complain:
I discovered Atlantis.

It's a relief to wake up
just before dying.

I turn sideways comfortably
when wars break out.

I am, but am not forced to be,
a child of this age.

Some years ago
I saw two suns.

And the day before yesterday a penguin.
I saw it quite clearly.

The open story

The world is never ready
for the coming of a child.

Our ships have not returned from Vinland yet.
We must still cross St Gotthard's Pass ahead.
We must outwit the guards in the desert of Thor,
crawl through the sewers to central Warsaw,
find a way to contact King Harald
and wait until Minister Fouché falls.
Only in Acapulco
shall we start again.

The supplies of dressings, clubs and water have run out.
We have neither lorries, nor the king's support.
The skinny horse will not buy us a sheriff.
There is no news of the Tartar's captives.
We do not have a warmer cave for winter
nor anyone who can speak Harari.

We do not know who to trust in Ninevah,
what the Prince-Cardinal will say,
whose names are listed in Beria's files.
They say that Charles the Great will strike at dawn.
So let us appease Cheops,
give ourselves up,
change our faith,
let's pretend to be friendly with the Doge
and deny connections with the Kwabe tribe.

It is time to make fire.
Let's call on grandma from Zabierzow
and unfasten the straps on our yurtas.

May the child birth be easy
and the baby grow well.
May she sometimes be happy
and leap across chasms.
May her heart be true
and her sharp mind range far.

But not so far
as to see the future.
Heavenly powers
spare her this gift.

Urszula Kozioł
(born 1931)

Urszula Kozioł was born in a small village near Bilgoraj (South East Poland). She studied humanities at the University of Wrocław and took her first degree in 1953. Her application for a place on a graduate course was turned down on political grounds and Kozioł was sent to teach in several provincial secondary schools. Due to the political relaxation following Stalin's death in 1953, she was allowed to go back to Wrocław and resume her graduate studies. Her first volume of poetry entitled *Gumowe klocki* (Blocks of Rubber) appeared in 1957. In the 1960s she returned to teaching and only in 1971 she was appointed co-editor of the well-known literary periodical 'Odra'. Since then Urszula Kozioł has been writing narrative prose, plays and literary essays. She has worked with Wrocław Students' Theatre and has written for Polish Radio. Her poetry and dramatic works have been published in Holland, Germany, Italy, Czechoslovakia, Denmark and Yugoslavia. Urszula Kozioł lives and works in Wroclaw.

Major editions of Kozioł's works:

Wybor wierszy (Selected poems), Warszawa 1976.
Poezje wybrane (Selected poems), Warszawa 1985.
Milne Holton, Paul Vangelisti, The New Polish Poetry, Pittsburg 1978.

Urszula Kozioł

A meat recipe

All you need is a knife,
all you need is a smooth stone.
You caress stone with blade until the rock gives in.
The knife should be noiseless, supple, shiny,
it should absorb rough tenderness and the nerves of
                                            hands.
After that it is quite simple.
A chopping-block, a pinch of salt,
greenery to taste to look good
and a bay-leaf.
After that it is quite ordinary
because only the spices matter
(Oh, think of a bowl and pretty colours!)
Fire is easy thanks to Prometheus.
Only the knife and the stone are essential
And one submissive neck.

A return to not knowing

It is time to return to not knowing.
We the onlookers
are being watched again.
We keep silent.
We have said too much.
Let us listen.
Soon we will all be asked to talk.

Our transparent faces
far from touch
hover on the paths of air.
Numbers vibrate, severed from dimension.
There are still loads with no weight.

What listens to us when we do not know
what dreams of us when we grope through day
what looks at us, directs us and records
when we believe we are alone?

It is time to return to not knowing.
Repeated
greetings from fallen snowmen
restive spaces
fire tree stone
a structure of dust
despair and hope.

Hypernakedness

My refuge was in the forest
— you have already cut it down.
I left for other places
— and they have become yours too.
Wherever I ran
you crossed my path.
Forewarned houses lurked at the crossroads.

It should have been a duel
but you had helpers.
Now they all hunt one creature,
no close season
no choice of weaponry.

There is no-one to give a shelter
no-one to keep a secret
no-one who would not point me out
no-one who would not track me down.
And you follow my footprints
before my desperate feet can press them in.

What's left to me is shut in a silent word,
but you have wormed into my secret self
and I am not my ally any more.
Though my tongue stays speechless
my guts open their hundred lips.
I am betrayed by glands and my breath denies me,
blood pulse and heart beat prepare my end.

You have taken so much. Though something still remains.
If you must have that too — take my death.
My last refuge is with her.

Urszula Kozioł

A thousand and one nights

We know it will come
We match plastic blocks,
sweet lies, petty thoughts

We know it will come

balloons — trivial words
rise up
boasting of colours

we know —

Scheherazade telling stories
tried to live one more day.

From a journey

In the labyrinth
where at every turn a woman
wields a ball of thread
trying to tempt
with a fresh colour

I bought
a needle, a thimble, some wool to try.
I wind it off.
Will there be enough
to darn a hole on a hero's heel
enough to twist round my finger
enough to . . .

No, not enough.

So here I am amongst you
in the labyrinth
where all threads are too short, except
threads spun by Alpha, except
threads spun by Beta, except
threads spun by threads
which are now in short supply.
I wind it off.
Is there enough for just one stitch
to prove I was led this way.

No, not enough.

So here I am
in the labyrinth
where another Ariadne holds out her ball
or something like her ball, or
something instead

Perhaps that instead
can help with this instead

No, not enough.

So here I am amongst you
in the labyrinth
And this wall is not a wall
but a wall of a wall
And this path is not a path
but a path of a path
And this sign scratched on brick
is a sign to nowhere
just a sign of a sign

how it stinks here
of sweaty waiting and real sweat
how shuffling feet
echo and re-echo in this place

now let us hold hands
let us hold on tight
let us stretch out and look
round the same old corner
round
another one, a bit further
round
the one that is *next*

nothing to be afraid of
and besides
there is no other labyrinth within
this labyrinth

nothing to be afraid of
and besides
all that is in the other place, not here,
all this is in the other place, there.

Spring relief

I'm glad that you can cope without me, Spring,
that you have your moments of leaves and reeds,
your grey skies and landscapes,
— everything proceeding just as it should,
without, thank God, any help from me.

Trees and flies proliferate by themselves,
light and shadow blend in their own design,
cunning beasts call out to other beasts
and nothing ever asks for my permission.

It's a relief to me that you, the earth,
can serve a universe and stay on course
without a thought for trying something new,
although it could be fun to be amazed!

I am excused from writing of seasons' change,
migrating birds, rivers in flood, the wind.
What a relief. The world can go on without me,
it can go on without me
child of Eve.

Urszula Kozioł

Summer

Is this my noon or my twilight?
I hear them coming for me,
the horseshoes of hours strike.

I wanted to bend the day
like a branch in someone's garden,
but day bent me like a branch of his own.

Halina Poświatowska
(1935–1967)

Halina Poświatowska was born in Częstochowa. She studied philosophy at the Jagiellonion University in Krakow. In 1958 Poświatowska went to the United States to undergo heart surgery. During her prolonged stay in the United States she continued her studies at Smith College, Northampton. On her return to Poland she was appointed lecturer in philosophy at the Jagiellonian University, but much of her time was spent in hospitals and medical centres. Poświatowska died in 1967. Between 1958 and 1967 she published three volumes of poetry.

Major editions of Poswiatowska's works:

Wiersze wybrane (Selected poems), Krakow 1980.

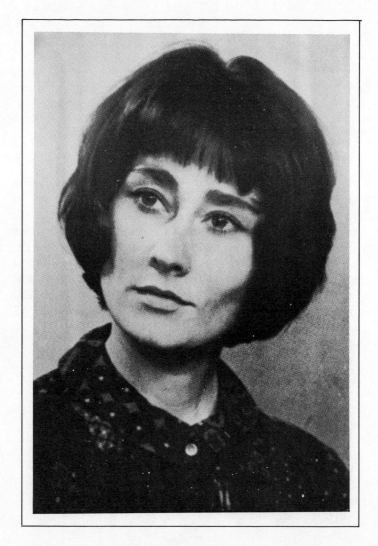

Halina Poświatowska

Whenever I really want to live I cry
and if life tries to leave me
I hold on to him
I say — Life
don't leave me yet

holding his warm hand in mine
my lips whispering
in his ear

Life
— as if life were a lover
sneaking away —

I throw myself on him
crying

If you leave me I'll die.

Halina Poświatowska

These words have always existed
in the open smile of a sunflower
on the black wing of a rook
and also
at the threshold of a slightly open door

as if there were no door
they'd exist
in the twigs of any tree

but you want
me to keep them just for myself
me to become
a rook's wing, a birch tree in summer
you want
me to sound
like a beehive open to the sun

you fool
I cannot own these words
I borrow them
from bees, from sun, from wind.

Argument pro

Eliot
is seductive with his pessimism
you can clearly see this
in anthologies of contemporary poetry
pessimism is spreading rapidly,
it takes hold of minds
like grass on the surface of soil

The rightness of this view
is strengthened by mirrors
by the surface of stagnant water,
reflecting a change of seasons
dynamism of nature
that decomposes instantly

an individual
counts no more than a leaf
swaying on a tree
it is hard to say
what her role is
she just exists for a while
feels
thinks

against immeasurable depth of water

you can see this in anthologies of contemporary poetry
and
in the eyes of people
who are just over thirty.

I still put curl papers in my hair
and kisses — birds of passage —
still perch on my lips
before flying south.
Summer is shorter these days
and cooler.

I still smile at myself in the mirror
Take it easy — I say — fire,
I must light the fire, buy the bread,
read Plato.
One has to think of tomorrow.

The air still turns silver
whenever I smile.
A tiny cloud quivers briefly then dissolves
and nothing is left,
not a smile or a thought of tomorrow
or the touch of a living hand.

Ewa Lipska
(born 1945)

Ewa Lipska was born in Krakow. She wrote her first poem at fifteen and won several prizes for young writers. In 1963 she was admitted to the Academy of Fine Arts in Krakow where she studied art history and painting. For years she published very little and belonged to none of the literary groups flourishing in the 1960s. Her first volume of poetry entitled *Wiersze* (Poems) appeared in 1967. Since then, Lipska has published more than five volumes of poetry and won several literary awards, including the Robert Graves Foundation Prize (1978). She travels widely, and in 1976 spent six months in the United States. Her American impressions are given in *Piąty zbiór wierszy* (Fifth Volume of Poetry, 1978). Lipska's poems have been translated into the major European languages. She lives in Krakow and co-edits the literary periodical *Pismo*.

Major editions of Lipska's works:

Wiersze (Poems), Warszawa 1967.
Dom Spokojnej Młodosci (The House of Peaceful Youth), Warszawa 1979.
Poezje wybrane (Selected poems), Warszawa 1981.

Ewa Lipska

Manifesto

Gods of the world unite!
Set up the party of one heart and liver,
And save the milkman
who at the crack of dawn
milks the morning mist
and whistles the tune about freedom.

If God exists

If God exists
I'll have dinner at his house.
Red berries instead of light.
He'll send his angel-chauffeur for me.
Clouds like fat doves
will flutter round the table.
We'll drink from empty vessels
vintage holy water and free will.

Even if God has stubby fingers
he still sucks them for eternity.
If God's a polyglot
he'll translate holy verse
for an anthology that's even holier
than the first word's drop
from which a river sprang.

Then God and I will ride our bikes
over a cherry tree, over the fields of paradise.
Earthly reeds in urns.
Predators lying fallow.

Then God will get off his bike and say
that it is he
who is God.
He'll take out his binoculars. He'll tell me
to look at the world. He'll explain
how it came into being,
how long he has gone on like this and
how unerringly he has erred with this world,
throwing ideas into the wind like paper planes.
If God is a believer
he'll pray to himself for life everlasting.
Oxen lift up the sun on their horns.
The table totters on its legs.
I'll get some medicine from God
and recover
right after my death.

On war

War is within us.
We are born with war.
The first scream.
The first fury.
Veins cannot hold in the blood.

And when we stand where roads cross
and when we love where war pauses
— we cling more tightly to this earth of ours.
We try to sink into earth. Into our mother.
We want our names to be remembered.
And we say too much
though we have no words.

So the earth, my Earth, roars around me.
And even if I could hide my eyes with trees,
and even if I could flee to desert isles,
and even if I could keep silent —
death
would still be there before me.
Lusting for victory, we rush on
to the unknown face of Maybe.

In my heart, I despair of this damned fate,
tired of studying graphs of theories
I shut my eyes. These woods of Academe are scented.
But even there, servile heroes emerge
hauling their shining armour in their arms.
They bring the shriek of war. It sets the tree on fire.
Here is the corpse of a bird. It sang a while ago.
The landscape's crushed its frame,
the panes shake, glass like old age shatters.

That shining, heavy armour. I am given a sword.
I run to the earth through the altered trees.
I am making a name for myself, no other name
will defeat this one of mine . . .
That is how every child who builds a sandcastle
learns about war
That is how every child who wields a wooden sword
knows about war.

Children

Children meet at nostalgic dinner-parties.
Children meet in executive sessions.
Children are experienced.
Some of them cannot recognize a swan.

Children have identity papers. Birth certificates.
Health records. Certificates of death.
Children choose their leaders who
make speeches praising rocking horses.

Children hijack planes and kidnap ministers.
Children emigrate to the ends of earth.
Children submit reports about their parents.
Children fight for the rights of wooden dolls.
Children sit in astrakhan fur coats.
Pink cakes fly through the air.
Children recall the fallen Roman Empire
and nod their little heads.

In the huge kindergarten of nations
children play ball and
spit cherry stones at each other.
They switch on an artificial sun
that rises like a mitigating circumstance.
Then children put aside their toys
and start to produce
some new children.

Witness

Anything I say
may be used in evidence.

Memory and facts —
two roads that diverge.

I do not remember
if it was dark or light.
If the road curved.

Who ran out first
and under which sentence.

I do not remember
if he was blinded by light,
or enlightened by reason.

If he fled from the scene of the crime
to the place of salvation.

If it was too late to plead to God
or too early to spread the news.

Truth and truth only
died in that accident.

Out from the judge's sleeve
leaped a live squirrel.

Ewa Lipska

On shores

The sea swallows clouds, violins and Magellan's
islands, ships coffers mothers and children
captains ear-rings shoes buttons and bows
despair and fears forks family photographs
shrieks and air.

On shores the relatives stand waiting for years.
Dressed in black. With flowers.
They throw pebbles into the liquid grave
and letters attached to the stones.

Down in the sea they have finally come to their senses.
They are frantically building the post office. They receive
letters periodicals volumes of poetry by living poets.
They cut back jobs and dismiss people.

Some steer away and choose
to cultivate new states,
transparent and waterproof.
They keep accepting new ships and cruisers
captains buttons air and children
despair and forks and coffers and ear-rings.
The influx of influential souls is welcome.

And on shores the relatives stand waiting for years.

Questions at a poetry reading

What's your favourite colour?
Your happiest day?
Did any poem outrun your imagination?
Do you have any hope?
You frighten us.
Why is the sky black?
Who shot down time?
Was it an empty hand, a hat sailing
across the sea?
Why a wedding dress
with a funeral wreath?
Why hospital corridors
Instead of forest paths?
Why the past and not the future?
Do you have faith? or don't you?
You frighten us.
We fly from you.

I try to stop them flying
straight into the fire.

My loneliness

My loneliness completed her course of study.
She was punctual and worked hard.
They awarded her medals and distinctions.

The course is popular.
Thousands of readers walk through it
writing things down.
Crossing them out.

She is tired of ruling
like Frederick the Great.

She already has some pupils.
Timidly subservient.

My loneliness is public.
She nests down in her cage
with her feathers of silence torn out.

Other Titles from
FOREST BOOKS

Special Collection

THE NAKED MACHINE Selected poems of Matthías Johannessen.
Translated from the *Icelandic* by Marshall Brement. (Forest/
Almenna bokáfélagid)
0 948259 44 2 cloth £7.95   0 948259 43 4 paper £5.95   96 pages

ON THE CUTTING EDGE Selected poems of Justo Jorge Padrón.
Translated from the *Spanish* by Louis Bourne.
0 948259 42 6 paper £7.95   176 pages

ROOM WITHOUT WALLS Selected poems of Bo Carpelan.
Translated from the *Swedish* by Ann Borne.
0 948259 08 6 paper £6.95   144 pages. Illustrated

CALL YOURSELF ALIVE? The love poems of Nina Cassian.
Translated from the *Romanian* by Andrea Deletant and
Brenda Walker. Introduction by Fleur Adcock.
0 948259 38 8 paper £5.95.   96 pages. Illustrated

RUNNING TO THE SHROUDS Six sea stories of
Konstantin Stanyukovich.
Translated from the *Russian* by Neil Parsons.
0 948259 04 3 paper £5.95   112 pages. Illustrated

East European Series

FOOTPRINTS OF THE WIND Selected poems of Mateja Matevski.
Translated from the *Macedonian* by Ewald Osers.
Introduction by Robin Skelton.
0 948259 41 8 paper £6.95   96 pages. Illustrated

FIRES OF THE SUNFLOWER Selected poems by Ivan Davidkov.
Translated from the *Bulgarian* by Ewald Osers.
0 948 259 48 5 paper £6.95   96 pages. Illustrated

POETS OF BULGARIA An anthology of contemporary
Bulgarian poets.
Edited by William Meredith. Introduction by Alan Brownjohn.
0 948259 39 6 paper £6.95   112 pages.

THE ROAD TO FREEDOM Poems by Geo Milev.
Translated from the *Bulgarian* by Ewald Osers.
UNESCO collection of representative works.
0 948259 40 X paper £6.95   96 pages. Illustrated

STOLEN FIRE Selected poems by Lyubomir Levchev.
Translated from the *Bulgarian* by Ewald Osers.
Introduction by John Balaban.
UNESCO collection of representative works.
0 948259 04 3 paper £5.95   112 pages. Illustrated

AN ANTHOLOGY OF CONTEMPORARY ROMANIAN POETRY
Translated by Andrea Deletant and Brenda Walker.
0 9509487 4 8 paper £5.00   112 pages.

GATES OF THE MOMENT Selected poems of Ion Stoica.
Translated from the *Romanian* by Brenda Walker and
Andrea Deletant. Dual text with cassette.
0 9509487 0 5 paper £5.00   126 pages   Cassette £3.50 plus VAT

SILENT VOICES An anthology of contemporary Romanian women
poets. Translated by Andrea Deletant and Brenda Walker.
0 948259 03 5 paper £6.95   172 pages.

EXILE ON A PEPPERCORN Selected poems of Mircea Dinescu.
Translated from the *Romanian* by Andrea Deletant and
Brenda Walker.
0 948259 00 0 paper £5.95.   96 pages. Illustrated.

LET'S TALK ABOUT THE WEATHER Selected poems of Marin Sorescu.
Translated from the *Romanian* by Andrea Deletant and
Brenda Walker.
0 9509487 8 0 paper £5.95   96 pages.

THE THIRST OF THE SALT MOUNTAIN Three plays by Marin Sorescu
(Jonah, The Verger, and the Matrix).
Translated from the *Romanian* by Andrea Deletant and
Brenda Walker.
0 9509487 5 6 paper £6.95   124 pages. Illustrated

VLAD DRACULA THE IMPALER A play by Marin Sorescu.
Translated from the *Romanian* by Dennis Deletant.
0 948259 07 8 paper £6.95   112 pages. Illustrated

Fun Series

JOUSTS OF APHRODITE Erotic poems collected from the Greek
Anthology Book V.
Translated from the *Greek* into modern English by Michael Kelly.
0 948259 05 1 cloth £6.95   0 94825 34 5 paper £4.95   96 pages